The Onesimus Workshop:
Facilitator's Guide

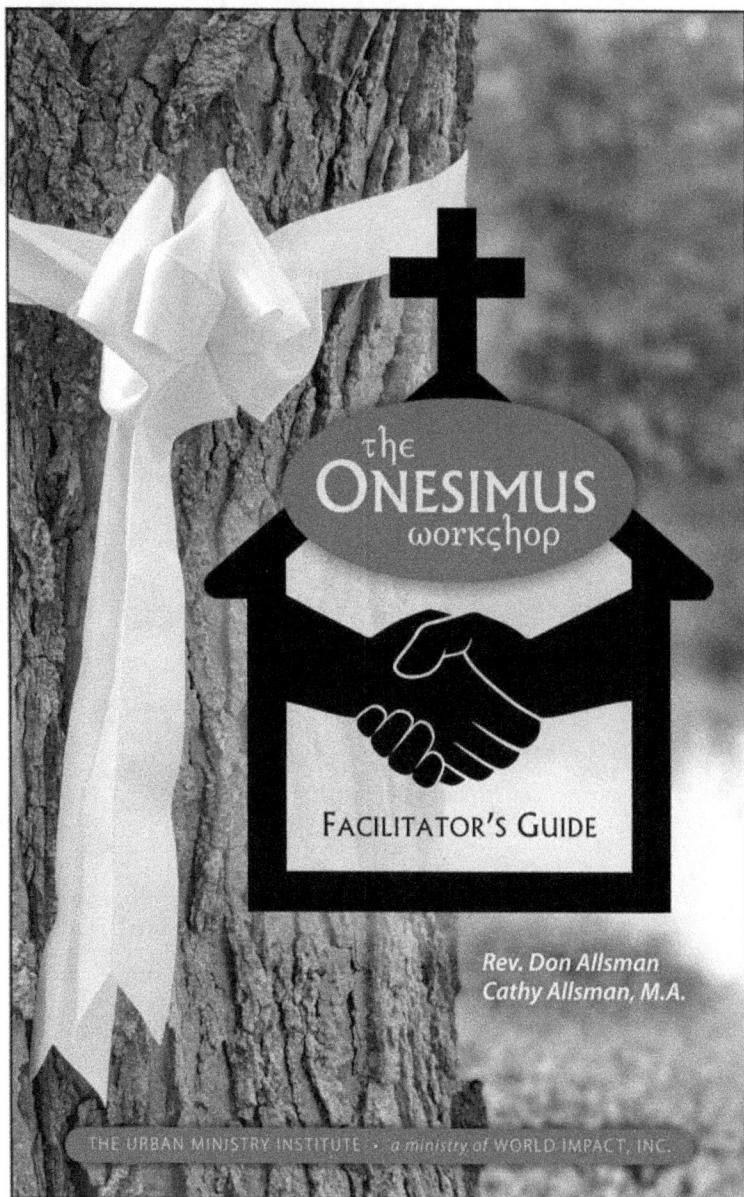

the
ONESIMUS
workshop

FACILITATOR'S GUIDE

Rev. Don Allsman
Cathy Allsman, M.A.

THE URBAN MINISTRY INSTITUTE · a ministry of WORLD IMPACT, INC.

TUMI Press
3701 East 13th Street North
Wichita, Kansas 67208

The Onesimus Workshop: Facilitator's Guide

The Urban Ministry Institute
3701 East 13th Street North
Wichita, KS 67208

ISBN: 978-1-62932-511-8

Published by TUMI Press
A division of World Impact, Inc.

The Urban Ministry Institute is a ministry of World Impact, Inc.

Table of Contents

Tips for Facilitation

Welcome to the Onesimus Workshop, as a workshop facilitator. This guide is intended to give you practical tips as you lead a workshop, using our video materials and workshop handbook. These are not requirements, but simply guides to help you design the best possible learning experience at your workshop.

The video sessions are packed with a lot of material, so you are strongly encouraged to use the "pause" button frequently to interject a brief comment or ask a clarifying question. This will help the listeners stay engaged but also help them put the material into their context.

1. Make sure you commit each step to prayer. The enemy wants to discourage the healthy incorporation of former prisoners into productive churches. Do not ignore the schemes of the enemy throughout this process. Watch for discouragement, division, and any way he can get you to give up.

2. Watch the video presentations and read the workbook in their entirety, so you get a thorough understanding

of the material. Do this well before the workshop so
you can plan for any adjustments to schedule or
design additional content.

3. When you schedule the workshop, you are free to
    conduct it as fits the occasion. For example, you can
    conduct the whole workshop on a Saturday morning,
    split it over a Friday night-Saturday morning, have
    four sessions on successive Thursday nights, etc. The
    timing and structure is up to you.

4. Before you engage a church or ministry to hold this
    workshop, find out what you can about their situation,
    their background, their work inside and outside of
    prison. Anything you can learn about their context
    will help you be prepared.

5. As you invite churches to participate in this workshop,
    make sure you get the endorsement and support of
    the lead pastor. The Onesimus Workshop is based
    on a whole-church approach, not just for selected
    participants. Therefore, it is vital to get support from
    the church's leadership before proceeding. The ideal
    would be for the lead pastor to introduce the
    workshop, and be present for all of the sessions.

6. If the lead pastor (or other leader) opens the workshop,
    give an introduction and explanation about how this
    relationship developed. Give some context and history
    for people in attendance so they know the connection
    between you and the church, and why you were invited

to host this workshop. Don't assume they know why they are present.

7. Tell them up front what to expect. Tell them there are four sessions, with discussion questions, breaks, and let them know how the day(s) will flow.

8. As you use the *pause* button to interject comments and manage the flow of the video sessions, keep in mind that participants can sometimes ask distracting questions that take the group on unnecessary tangents that break momentum and cause frustration. As you utilize the *pause* button, make sure you keep in mind what your time schedule is so you can stay on task.

9. After the sessions or during breaks, you will likely receive many questions. Do not be afraid if you do not know all the answers. You don't have to be an expert, knowing the "right" answer to every query. It is ok to say, "I don't know, you might need to discover that as you go" or "I don't know but I think I know how I might get a good answer to that."

10. If you have experience to speak to a situation, feel free to share that experience. But be careful to qualify it as no more than your experience; others in the room may have different experiences with the same issue. Ministry among the incarcerated can vary widely from one institution to another, from county to county, from state to state, from federal prisons to state prisons. Be cautious in presenting experiences as facts.

11. One optional way to help participants get into the flow of the video sessions is to create discussion around a Case Study (see Appendix 3, *The Case for Case Studies*). This helps prime the participants to engage in the topic, and focuses their attention on the relevance of the video material they are about to watch. It stimulates their curiosity regarding the meaning of the topics about to be covered. We have included several possible Case Studies (see Appendix 1) that you can use, or you can create your own. If you include a Case Study at the beginning of each video session, make sure you manage the time so you don't get behind. You may have animated discussion that needs to be cut off in order to move into the video presentation.

12. For any discussion (a Case Study at the beginning or for the questions at the end of the session), consider breaking up into smaller groups if there are twelve or more people in attendance. If you have more than twelve people, you will not get full participation if you lead a single group discussion.

13. Make sure you leave time for discussion after the video presentation. People need to process what they have just heard, and it will be internalized and applied when it has been discussed first. They need time and dialogue in order to put into practice the implications in their setting. These issues are complex and people need interaction to develop their convictions about these matters.

14. Depending on how you structure the sessions, make sure people have water and snacks.

15. When most people think about reentry, they focus on helping former prisoners get jobs, housing, and other physical needs. Be aware that participants may want to take you off topic and focus on these issues. Keep them on topic, reminding them that the purpose of the Onesimus Workshop is to help them find friends, more than finding jobs or housing.

APPENDIX 1
Sample Case Studies

1. Sharon, a long-time friend from the church asks you to have coffee. After you exchange news about your families, she says, "Let me tell you why I wanted to talk. I've heard about this idea of letting prisoners come to our church and I'm concerned. Of course we should be open to anyone who wants to come, but what possible good could come from this? Why would we do this with all the dangers it could pose to the kids in the church? I just don't see the benefit of this." What would you say to this dear friend?

2. A missionary, supported by your church, sends your Sunday school class a video about how the Gospel is being preached and people are coming to Christ in that foreign country. But during the video, the members of the church are shown to be wearing traditional clothing worn by Muslims. After the video is over, one person raises their hand to ask, "If they are coming to Christ, why do they dress like Muslims?" How would you respond?

3. At dinner one night, your fourteen-year-old son says, "I saw this show on TV about prison, and it was scary. Can God change someone who has been a killer and been in prison all their life?" How would you respond?

4. One Sunday, your pastor gets up to deliver the message and says, "God has laid it on my heart that our congregation needs to be more welcoming to prisoners coming out of prison." At the next elder meeting, one of the elders says, "I can see the benefit of welcoming prisoners who are now Christians, but I am afraid that it will overrun our budget. We are barely surviving as it is. How can we afford to offer housing and meet the other needs that people have when they get out of prison?" As a fellow elder, what would you say?

5. At your Tuesday night Bible study, the topic of prison reform comes up in conversation. One of the people jokes, "All those people want is a free bed and three square meals." One of the other members jumps in and says, "You all don't know it but my son is a prisoner. I have never said anything because I am so ashamed. I can tell you that although he got on drugs and was sent to prison, he is walking with the Lord now and is not like what you are saying." What would you say in response?

6. During lunch with Jeremy, a co-worker at the office, you ask about his family. He says, "My son-in-law just got out of prison, and my daughter is having a difficult time in the adjustment. I just don't understand. How could it be difficult to go from prison to freedom?" What insights could you offer in response?

7. You watch a news story on TV where a former
    prisoner says the main reason his friends commit
    crimes and go back to prison is the lack of a job and
    education. But you find an article on the web that
    says having a job and education are not significant
    factors that lead to prisoners re-offending (also called
    "recidivism"). The article gives several other factors
    that lead to recidivism. How do you make sense of
    these conflicting reports?

8. Your mother calls you on the phone to catch up with
    your life. During the conversation, she mentions her
    friend Doris, who is trying to help a former prisoner
    get on her feet. She says, "I don't understand why this
    is taking so long. Doris has been helping this young
    lady for over three months now and it seems like she
    should be ready to be on her own." What insights
    could you share about this situation?

9. Your cousin Jim has been burdened by Matthew 25 and
    Jesus' command to care for the poor and for prisoners.
    Not having any background with prison ministry, Jim
    attends a seminar on helping prisoners with reentry.
    After the seminar, he phones you for advice, saying,
    "I went to the seminar thinking I should volunteer at
    a halfway house or something, but the people explained
    that what people need more than a program is a friend.
    I don't understand that. What can I do to help someone
    like that? I've never even been to a prison." What
    advice could you give to Jim?

10. Your sister Carla calls you one day in exasperation. "I volunteered to help a prisoner get situated after coming out of prison and she calls me day and night with problems that she could easily solve herself. She keeps asking for money and it seems like the more I give, the more she asks. There is no end in sight! I don't know why I said I would do this and I can't figure out how to get out of it!" What would you say to Carla?

11. You just started going with a group of men from your church to visit prisoners. One Saturday a month, you spend the morning teaching a Bible study and getting to know the men. One prisoner named Kevin tells you he is going to be released next month after three years of incarceration. When you ask him about his plans, he looks at you with a blank stare and says, "What do you mean?" You ask him, "What are going to do when you get out?" He says, "I don't know, I need to get a job I guess. I'll figure it out when I get out." You are astonished that he hasn't thought about what steps he is going to take. What should you say to Kevin?

12. You are a deacon at your church and a visitor approaches you after the service and asks, "What does the church do to train leaders to become deacons or elders or pastors?" You say, "I'm not sure." He says, "Ok. Well, what do you do to follow up a

new believer if I lead someone to Christ?" Again, you are not sure and say, "I don't know about that either." Other than defer to others in leadership, what might you do to shore up these deficiencies?

13. Your Uncle Phil gives you a book on the need for criminal justice reform, asking you to give your thoughts. Phil is intrigued by the challenge but is overwhelmed by it all. He feels like he can't do everything in the book, and there are so many needs, he is not sure what to do next, if anything. You read the book and there are eight ways to help prisoners in reentry, and each of them are valid. What would you say to Phil?

14. You are pastor of a church where Lance, one of your members, has been visiting the county jail for several years. Lance has been somewhat of a loner in this ministry but by all accounts it seems fruitful enough. Lance doesn't say much about it. Recently some people have shown up at church with Lance who appear to be unsavory characters; they have tattoos and have an intense manner to them. Others in the congregation have approached you and said, "Pastor, are you aware that Lance is bringing people to church who he met in jail?" How will you handle this?

APPENDIX 2
Sample Schedule

Here is a table that gives you an overview, using a Saturday morning schedule as an example:

Session 1: The Onesimus Vision

Time	Activity
8:00-8:30	Welcome/Case Study
8:30-9:05	Presentation (Video)
9:05-9:20	Discussion
9:20-9:25	Break/Transition to Session 2

Concept
See the Opportunity

Objectives
- Understand the background for the formation of the Onesimus vision.
- Appreciate the powerful effects of cultural differences.
- Recognize the amazing opportunity for your church to have trained, zealous leaders.

Content
- History of WI/TUMI
- Onesimus Vision
- The Opportunity of a Lifetime

Sample Schedule, continued

Session 2: Understanding Prison Culture

Time	Activity
9:25-9:35	Welcome/Case Study
9:35-10:10	Presentation (Video)
10:10-10:25	Discussion
10:25-10:30	Break/Transition to Session 3

Concept
Understand the Problem

Objectives
- Acknowledge your fears and appreciate fears that prisoners have.
- Understand what prisoners experience that is different from civilian life.
- Recognize the factors that lead to recidivism.

Content
- Hopes and Fears
- Prison Culture
- Jails vs. Prisons

Sample Schedule, continued

Session 3: The Process of Re-enculturation

Time	Activity
10:30-10:40	Welcome/Case Study
10:40-11:15	Presentation (Video)
11:15-11:25	Discussion
11:25-11:30	Break/Transition to Session 4

Concept
See the Solution

Objectives
- Understand the time and effort it will take to help a former prisoner adapt.
- Recognize the differences between a systemic approach and a programmatic approach.
- Appreciate the seven keys that will make the process successful.

Content
- Systemic vs. Programmatic Approach
- Myths about Helping Former Prisoners
- Seven Keys to Success

Sample Schedule, continued

Session 4: The Next Steps

Time	Activity
11:30-11:40	Welcome/Case Study
11:40-12:00	Presentation (Video)
12:00-12:15	Discussion
12:15	Conclude

Concept
Implement the Plan

Objectives
- Understand the tools World Impact offers.
- Outline the three essential next steps.
- Explain eight options for implementation.
- Decide which initial steps you will take.

Content
- The Tools WI Offers
- The Essential Steps
- Levels of Participation

APPENDIX 3

The Case for Case Studies

Rev. Dr. Don L. Davis

If you have ever taught or sat in a Capstone class, you have noticed the presence of "Contact" stories or the "Case Studies" sections of the lesson. These are ubiquitous (everywhere present) in Capstone; more than 450 cases are offered at the beginning or end of the lessons, positioned to either introduce the lesson or to dig into the meaning of the lesson's content, at the end. They are numerous in number and thorny in character. Many suggest that they never seem to allow for a clear, simple resolvable answer to the problems they pose. Why include Contact stories and Case Studies in the lessons, in the first place?

While it may not be immediately obvious, the answer to this question is important. Case Studies are life application stories which highlight the importance of connecting truth that is researched with life that is lived. These stories, whether invented or actual, allow the learners to explore the relationship between the truths they discovered in their Bible study, and the tough, difficult decisions which emerge in the midst of our life circumstances. The method of engaging Contact stories and Case Studies in Capstone flows from the ancient rabbinic method of discerning wisdom through connecting the biblical truth to the facts of particular cases, in the light of the shared wisdom of tradition. It is a sound, helpful approach to discover truth together in a learning cohort.

What Exactly Is a Case Study? A Biblical Example

In the context of the Capstone lesson, what exactly is a case? A case is a life application story that is either posed or described in the Contact or Case Study section of the material. It is based on biblical examples which reveal the ancient practice of careful observation of situations, and the corresponding act of making generalizations and discovering principles after you have observed and analyzed a particular situation.

A clear biblical example of this practice is given in Proverbs 24.30-34 (ESV):

> I passed by the field of a sluggard, by the vineyard of a man lacking sense, [31] and behold, it was all overgrown with thorns; the ground was covered with nettles, and its stone wall was broken down. [32] Then I saw and considered it; I looked and received instruction. [33] A little sleep, a little slumber, a little folding of the hands to rest, [34] and poverty will come upon you like a robber, and want like an armed man.

Note the order of this investigation: first, careful, critical consideration is made of a particular situation (i.e., a case). This situation is noted carefully, looking at the various facts and conditions associated with it. (This is important: cases are built on a careful knowledge of the facts of the situation). Next, the observer reflects on the *meaning* of what he sees; he considers it, looks at it, and then "*receives instruction.*" Finally, the observer, after gathering the facts of the situation and reflecting on their meaning, generalizes a principle, a truth, that can be used not only to understand the case under investigation, but other cases of similar kind that may arise. "A little sleep, a little slumber, a little folding of the hands to rest, and poverty will come upon you like a robber, and want like an armed man."

Notice how this process of case study dovetails into the discovery of a biblical insight or principle that is listed in the form of a "proverb," a short, pithy, memorizable statement that summarizes the insight received from the observation and reflection. Of course, to test the generalization, other cases can be consulted, and the principle applied to them, to see if similar results are discovered. Still, the process is clear: observation, interpretation, generalization, decision.

Of special interest here is the connection of cases to rabbinic methods of truth seeking and truth telling. Case study is an ancient, rabbinic way to discern God's truth and will in a difficult and/or controversial situation.

Case Studies and Rabbinic Methods of Wisdom
A clear biblical example arises from the case of Gamaliel in his comment on the Sanhedrin's thoughts regarding the apostles. He demonstrated this ancient rabbinic practice in his response to the Sanhedrin Council's determination to kill Peter and the apostles (Acts 5.33-39). After hearing Peter and the apostles' courageous defense against the Council's threat for them to be quiet and to cease speaking of Jesus of Nazareth, they wanted to kill them, presumably for blasphemy and false teaching among the people.

On hearing this, Gamaliel warned the Council not to act on such a decision, and made an argument to them based on his working knowledge of relevant cases dealing with the futility of rebellious movements to succeed or sustain in the face of God's judgments.

Gamaliel then referred to two cases which illumined the situation they were facing with the apostles. The first dealt with Theudas with his 400 insurrectionists, whose rebellious cause produced his own death, the dispersal of his followers, and the total elimination of his movement (Acts 5.36). The second involved Judas the Galilean whose rebellion rose up during the days of the census, and drew some folk after him. (Josephus the historian actually gives a comprehensive account of his actions.) Like Theudas, Gamaliel says, Judas perished, and everyone who followed him was scattered as well (Acts 5.37).

After considering the lessons associated with these cases, Gamaliel makes his argument based on the principle gleaned from his observation of the cases of Theudas and Judas.

> "So in the present case I tell you, keep away from these men and let them alone, for if this plan or this undertaking is of man, it will fail; but if it is of God, you will not be able to overthrow them. You might even be found opposing God!" So they took his advice.
> ~ Acts 5.38-39

Although the Council decided to not kill the apostles, they did unfortunately foolishly and unjustifiably beat the apostles and charged them not to speak any more in the name of the Lord Jesus (vv. 40-41).

Gamaliel's approach in this situation should be seen as a rabbinic tested method of dealing with difficult and controversial problems and issues. He related the particular situation of Peter and the apostles to a bigger picture of the futility of rebellious movements. When confronted with a problem that called for a conclusive, biblical answer, Gamaliel immediately referred to two relevant cases judged to be of the same subject. He recited the cases, summarized his findings from his reflections on them, and then generalized a principle that related directly to what they ought to consider with the apostles in their situation, right then and there. This method of Gamaliel was a standard rabbinic approach to applying Scripture to life – observation of the facts of a case, reflection on other related, relevant cases, the generalization of a principle, and connecting that principle to life.

Historically speaking, a rabbi was a "keeper of the cases and their interpretations" for the community, in sync with the traditions of the elders. As a student-pastor-counselor of the tradition, he could draw from his internal storehouse the various cases and their relevant biblical principles to the different issues of life that were brought to him. As he encountered situations, he would reflect on the facts, and relate those to the law and to tradition's understanding of it. His duty was to be as aware as possible of the body of cases and their corollary biblical principles which related to various questions or concerns as they would come up. The rabbi was trained in assessing relevant and appropriate cases and relating them to the Law and to tradition. In any given question, what were the relevant cases, or the "seminal" (precedent setting) cases connected to it?

What were the "opposite" or "contrary" cases that reveal a breaking of the principle under consideration? What might be considered either "borderline" or "hybrid" cases, those stories containing elements that were hard to categorize, both puzzling and difficult to ascertain?

In the same way the rabbis were equipped to relate the truth of the Scripture to actual cases and historical instances, so we hope our students, through the use of the Contacts and Case Studies, will be better outfitted to relate their learning to real life happenings.

Case Studies and Communities of Learning

In a similar vein, Case Studies also offer a community of learning (like a module cohort) a solid, testable approach to discovering and applying truth together, as a group.

Case approaches assume the priority of the community's reflection and interaction with life over time. Through its own told and lived history, a community builds up shared knowledge which it trusts, has tested, and shares with its members. This knowledge is codified in principles, and passed down generation to generation through tradition and shared insight. These "insights" gleaned over time must still be tested and proven by experience, but the method and process is solid. Cases are considered, observed, interpreted. Principles are discovered and tested in experience. These principles are then cherished, learned, and used to make decisions in difficult situations, and to set direction in carrying out what we believe God's will to be in a given circumstance.

As we think about this, we ought not be too abstract. The easiest way to think together is to tell stories and interpret them together. Case Studies should be seen as stories (whether invented or historical) that enable a community to wrestle with its commitments in the context of a real experience. Stories are the heart of our lives together as communities. We live in actual situations which, when we speak of them, take the shape of specific stories we share.

A story makes the truth come alive; it forces us to think about the meaning of what we have learned in a way that actually impacts our lives and our circumstances. Cases become living pictures, the kind that are worth a thousand words, and help us draw out the wisdom that it invites us to see and apply. More than this, Case Studies invite a community to connect its research, its problems, and its opportunities to real truths.

In a nutshell, Case Study dialogue in a group forces all participants to share their observations and findings, and allows the group to engage in its members' thoughts and reflections. Because of this shared nature of Case Study, it forces those in a group to be convinced but less dogmatic in asserting the finality of their individual opinions and judgments with others. Case Study is therefore difficult; it can be hard to see the facts the same way, or even weigh the same facts in the same manner. To explore cases sometimes requires much time and open dialogue among those engaging the stories with the truth.

Even in light of these challenges, though, Case Studies are highly effective in training members to both listen and reflect together. Other members will emphasize things we do not, and they will offer different interpretations on the meaning of the facts we discover. We must learn to learn together, and not abstractly. Case Studies call the learners to connect their knowledge with actual life situations, and forces the researchers to become problem-solvers, counselors, and deliberators together. The insights gleaned are gleaned by us together. The Case Study becomes the lens by which we together discover truth and relate it to life. Cases provide data, but also emotion, insight, and wisdom. There's no better method of biblical counseling than using Case Studies to explore God's will.

Case Studies: Tell the Stories and Learn Together

In conclusion, Case Studies are demanding, but properly understood and engaged, they provide an open-ended, communal approach and strategy toward effective life application of truth. Allocate your lesson engagement time blocks to generously give as much time as you can to both the Contact and Case Study sections of the Capstone lesson. Carefully review the facts and issues introduced in the various cases, and prayerfully discern which ones you will concentrate on, what principles you will explore, and what other relevant cases you might discuss.

Also, realize that the Contacts and Case Studies are offered to give you a ready-made platform to test your students' abilities to relate the truth to life, to connect principles with practice. This is "on-the-job training" for Christian leadership, without the horrible consequences of their poor or unjustified decisions! Allow the Case Studies to be the testing zone of how your students relate the insights of the Scripture to the challenges of real life situations.

Do not forget that Case Studies do not lend themselves to "right/wrong" kinds of dualistic approaches. Their observation of the facts, reflection on their meaning, and generalizing of principles will neither be easy nor clean. However, the lessons they learn in how to approach the tough issues of life will be invaluable. Even if the answers do not always resolve into "the one right answer," it will be heartening to see that there may be more than one "right answer!" (God tells husbands to love their wives as Christ does the church, but he does not tell them to all buy flowers and have a date night on the third Sunday of each month! The command is clear, but we have freedom in how we apply the command to a particular situation [2 Cor. 3.17].)

Continuing in the Word of Christ as his disciples demands that we relate his Word to our lives (John 8.31-32). Let us never neglect the cases of our own lives, and the ways in which the Scripture can make us wise to salvation in Christ, in the very center of our days as we live them (2 Tim. 3.15-17).

www.ingramcontent.com/pod-product-compliance
Lightning Source LLC
Chambersburg PA
CBHW060548030426
42337CB00021B/4493